# School Rules!

Nina Tsang

Rigby®

A Harcourt Achieve Imprint

www.Rigby.com
1-800-531-5015

# Hi, I'm Ella.
This week we learned about rules at school.

**RULES**

- Keep your hands and feet to yourself.
- Follow directions.
- Walk, don't run.
- Help others.
- Take turns and share.
- Clean up your area.
- Be a good listener.

My teacher gave us books to help us remember the rules, even when we're not at school.

After school, Mommy
picked me up.
Sam tried to pinch me!

I told him, "Keep your hands and feet to yourself! That's a rule I learned in school."

Keep your hands and feet to yourself.

Mommy said to hold hands
and wait to cross the street.
But Sam was too busy picking
flowers to hold my hand.

I told him, "Follow directions!
That's a rule I learned
in school."

Follow directions.

We stopped at the bank
on our way home.
Sam ran to get a lollipop.

I told him, "Walk, don't run! That's a rule I learned in school."

Walk, don't run.

When we got home,
I set the dinner table.
Sam watched TV.

I told him, "Help others!
That's a rule I learned
in school."

Help others.

During dinner, Sam tried
to grab the bowl of
peas from me.

I told him, "Take turns and share!
That's a rule I learned in school."

Take turns and share.

13

After dinner, I carried
my dishes to the sink.
Sam left his dishes out.

I told him, "Clean up your area.
That's a rule I learned in school."

Clean up your area.

At story time, I told Sam to be a good listener. But he was already asleep!

Be a good listener.